ULTIMATE CARS

BMW

Published in 2011 by The Rosen Publishing Group Inc.
29 East 21st Street, New York, NY 10010

First Edition

Editor: Camilla Lloyd
Produced by Tall Tree Ltd
Editor, Tall Tree: Emma Marriott
Designer: Jonathan Vipond

Library of Congress Cataloging-in-Publication Data

Colson, Rob Scott.
    BMW / by Rob Scott Colson. -- 1st ed.
        p. cm. -- (Ultimate cars)
    ISBN 978-1-4488-3087-9 (trade paperback Lamborghini/BMW)
    1. BMW automobiles--Juvenile literature. I. Title.
    TL215.B25C638 2011
    629.222'2--dc22

                                    2009045416

Photographs
All images BMW AG, except:
4 Lothar Spurzem

Manufactured in China
CPSIA Compliance Information: Batch #WAS0102PK: For Further Information
contact Rosen Publishing, New York, New York at 1-800-237-9932

ULTIMATE CARS

BMW

Rob Scott Colson

PowerKiDS
press™

New York

BMW

BMW (Bavarian Motor Works) is a car company based in Munich, Germany. The company began by making aircraft engines during World War I.

Banned from making aircraft after Germany lost the war, BMW changed to making motorcycles, which it still does today. The company started making cars in 1928. BMW now makes a range of cars that are high performance, which means that they reach very fast top speeds.

Amazing Design

In 2004, BMW opened its new Virtual Reality Room. This advanced computer system allows engineers to handle new designs before they have been built. A visor enables them to look at a 3-D image of a new engine part or control. Wearing special gloves, they experience what it would be like to operate the new part. In this way, they can better understand and even improve how it will work.

The 319/1, first made in 1935, was a stylish, 2-seater convertible.

On the Racetrack

BMW has raced its cars and motorcycles in motor sports since the 1930s. Drivers compete in Formula 1, the biggest competition for cars, with the team BMW Sauber, and they won their first race at the Canadian Grand Prix in 2008. The company also runs its own competition for young drivers called Formula BMW.

The BMW 328 was a sports car made between 1937 and 1939. It was driven in many races around Europe, and won the British RAC Rally in 1939.

Z4 Roadster

The Z4 Roadster is a 2-seater sports car that came into production in 2002. It has a very long hood that covers a powerful 3.2-liter engine, and the driver sits toward the back. This gives the car a very distinctive shape.

The Z4's shape ensures that weight is evenly distributed across all four wheels, which helps the car to accelerate quickly. The Z4 can go so fast that BMW have limited its speed to 155 mph (250 kph).

Amazing Design

A roadster—also known as a convertible—is a car with a soft roof that can be retracted (pulled back) in fine weather. The roof of the Z4 is operated electrically, and is one of the fastest retractable roofs in the world. At the push of a button, it pulls back in just 10 seconds to let the driver and passenger feel the wind in their hair.

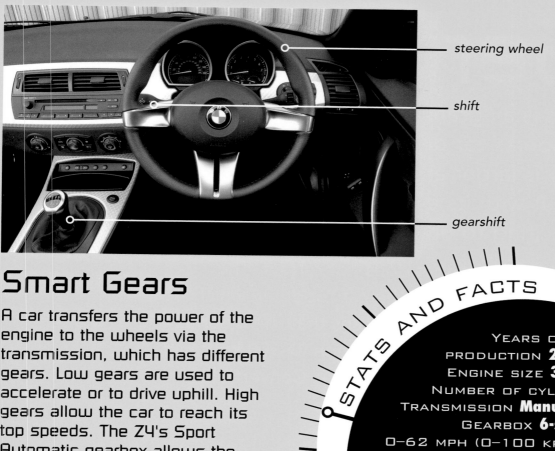

steering wheel

shift

gearshift

Smart Gears

A car transfers the power of the engine to the wheels via the transmission, which has different gears. Low gears are used to accelerate or to drive uphill. High gears allow the car to reach its top speeds. The Z4's Sport Automatic gearbox allows the driver to change gear using either the gearshift or a shift behind the steering wheel. If they prefer, they can also let the car change gears automatically.

STATS AND FACTS

YEARS OF PRODUCTION **2002–08**
ENGINE SIZE **3.2 liter**
NUMBER OF CYLINDERS **6**
TRANSMISSION **Manual/automatic**
GEARBOX **6-speed**
0–62 MPH (0–100 KPH) **5.7 seconds**
TOP SPEED **Limited to 155 mph (250 kph)**
WEIGHT **3,053 lb. (1,385 kg)**
CO_2 EMISSIONS (G/KM) **292**
FUEL ECONOMY
32.8 mpg (8.6 L/100 km)

6 Series Coupé

The 6 Series is a "grand tourer," which means that it is a sports car designed to drive long distances. It is larger and heavier than the Z4 Roadster, but with its enormous engine, it is just as exciting to drive.

A coupé has a hard roof that does not retract. The roof of a coupé helps to hold the car together, which improves its performance. This means that the 6 Series Coupé can accelerate from 0 to 62 mph (0–100 kph) half a second more quickly than the 6 Series Convertible.

The high-tech headrests save many a stiff neck. In the event of a crash, they move forward to prevent the driver's or passenger's head from jerking backward, which can cause a neck injury called whiplash.

Amazing Design

The 6 Series Coupé is fitted with "Night Vision," which uses infrared sensors to detect heat-producing objects, such as pedestrians or animals, up to 328 yards (300 m) away. An image is displayed on the iDrive screen inside the car, so the driver knows someone is there before they can see them. This extra second might just save a life.

The iDrive screen shows information from the car's on-board computer.

Light but Strong

To stand up to long journeys, a grand tourer needs to be strong and reliable. But adding strength also adds weight, which makes the car slower. The 6 Series Coupé's chassis (its "skeleton") is made of high-tech material that is both strong and light. The roof is made of lightweight carbon fiber, which lowers the car's center of gravity, making it easier to control at high speeds.

STATS AND FACTS

YEARS OF PRODUCTION **2007–present**
ENGINE SIZE **4.8 liter**
NUMBER OF CYLINDERS **8**
TRANSMISSION **Manual/automatic**
GEARBOX **6-speed**
0–62 MPH (0–100 KPH) **5.1 seconds**
TOP SPEED **Limited to 155 mph (250 kph)**
WEIGHT **3,803 lb. (1,725 kg)**
CO_2 EMISSIONS (G/KM) **279**
FUEL ECONOMY **24.1 mpg (11.7 L/100 km)**

M3

The M3 is a compact 4-seater designed for driving on roads and the racetrack. It can accelerate from 0 to 62 mph (0–100 kph) in under 5 seconds.

The M3's engine is the key to its speed. The engine block—the heart of the engine in which the pistons pump up and down—is built by the same team that builds the engine block for the BMW Sauber Formula 1 car.

Amazing Design

Four exhaust pipes pump the waste gas produced by the M3's engine out into the air. Car exhaust fumes are a major source of pollution, so each pipe is fitted with a device called a catalytic converter. The converters contain special chemicals known as catalysts. The catalysts react with the most harmful gases, such as carbon monoxide and nitrogen oxide, and turn them into safer gases, such as carbon dioxide and nitrogen.

STATS AND FACTS

YEARS OF PRODUCTION **2005–present**
ENGINE SIZE **4 liter**
NUMBER OF CYLINDERS **8**
TRANSMISSION **Manual/automatic**
GEARBOX **6-speed**
0–62 MPH (0–100 KPH) **4.8 seconds**
TOP SPEED **Limited to 155 mph (250 kph)**
WEIGHT **3,649 lb. (1,655 kg)**
CO_2 EMISSIONS (G/KM) **279**
FUEL ECONOMY **22.8 mpg (12.4 L/100 km)**

The backs of the M3's door mirrors are shaped to point into the wind and ease the air around them.

Aerodynamic Shape

As a car moves, it is slowed down by the air it is pushing against, known as air resistance. Every part of the M3 is designed to ensure that the air flows smoothly around it, reducing air resistance. Engineers test different shapes in wind tunnels to refine their aerodynamics (how they move through the air).

E23 7 Series

Launched in 1977, the E23 7 Series came equipped with the very latest gadgets.

E23 drivers were truly pampered: the most expensive models included heated seats, an electric sunroof, and air conditioning. With top speeds of over 125 mph (200 kph), the E23 was no slouch, but its emphasis on comfort meant it didn't quite match its faster high-performance cousins.

The Hydrogen 7 fuels up with liquid hydrogen at a special filling station.

Amazing Design

In the early 1980s, BMW teamed up with the German Institute for Aviation and Space Flight to convert an E23 to run on liquid hydrogen rather than gasoline. This was the start of a long-term project to find an alternative source of energy for cars. After 25 years of development work, BMW launched the first-ever hydrogen-powered production car, the Hydrogen 7, in 2006.

STATS AND FACTS

YEARS OF PRODUCTION
1977–86
(this model 1981)
ENGINE SIZE **3.4 liter**
NUMBER OF CYLINDERS **6**
TRANSMISSION **Manual (Stick shift)**
GEARBOX **5-speed**
0–62 MPH (0–100 KPH) **7.3 seconds**
TOP SPEED **140 mph (225 kph)**
WEIGHT **3,505 lb. (1,590 kg)**
CO$_2$ EMISSIONS (G/KM) **Not available**
FUEL ECONOMY
25.7 mpg (11 L/100 km)

New Technology

The first 7 Series, which BMW codenamed the E23 Series, was fitted with the best technology of its time. This included a fuel-injected engine and an antilock braking system (ABS), which stops the wheels from locking while braking, preventing dangerous skids. These are standard features in cars today, but were rare in the 1970s.

507 Roadster

By the mid-1950s, BMW had lost its reputation as a manufacturer of fine 2-seater sports cars. The 507 Roadster was the model that would restore it.

The car's stylish, sleek shape was a hit among those who could afford it. The singer Elvis Presley bought one while he was serving in the U.S. army in Germany.

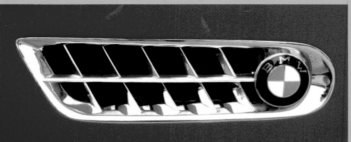

The 507's side air vents make the 507 instantly recognizable.

A Costly Car

Originally, BMW intended to make 5,000 cars per year. But even though the 507 sold for several thousand dollars—many years' salaries for the average worker—it cost even more to build, and each one lost BMW money. The 507 Roadster both restored BMW's reputation and drove it close to bankruptcy, and in the end, only 252 cars were made. Remarkably, half a century later, over 200 are still on the road somewhere in the world.

Amazing Design

The chassis for each 507 Roadster was modeled out of aluminum by hand, which means that no two are exactly the same. They came with an optional detachable hard top (roof), which was also made by hand, so that the hard top of one car would not fit any other.

STATS AND FACTS

YEARS OF PRODUCTION **1956–59**
ENGINE SIZE **3.2 liter**
NUMBER OF CYLINDERS **8**
TRANSMISSION **Manual (Stick shift)**
GEARBOX **4-speed**
0–62 MPH (0–100 KPH) **11 seconds**
TOP SPEED **122 mph (196 kph)**
WEIGHT **2,899 lb. (1,315 kg)**
CO_2 EMISSIONS (G/KM) **Not available**
FUEL ECONOMY
24 mpg (11.8 L/100 km)

Formula 1 Car

In 2006, BMW teamed up with the Swiss company Sauber to compete in Formula 1, the biggest motor sports event of all.

Formula 1 cars must meet a strict set of rules. For example, the engine must have 8 cylinders, be no bigger than 2.4 liters, and cannot be turbocharged. By limiting cars in this way, the race organizers ensure that teams have to come up with more efficient and competitive cars every year.

downshift (change to a lower gear)

screen displays information from the race marshals

upshift (change to a higher gear)

Amazing Design

The steering wheel is a Formula 1 driver's control center. With both hands on the wheel, they can work the clutch, change gear, talk to their team, and even take a drink. The wheel has a quick-release mechanism to allow the driver to climb out of the car in less than 5 seconds—which may save their life in a crash. This is driver Nick Heidfeld's wheel. The handles are made of silicon that has been molded to the exact shape of his hands.

clutch shift

Pit Stop

During a race, drivers come into the pits one or more times to change tires and refuel. The car is jacked off the ground, the wheels replaced, the tank filled with fuel, then lowered back down to rejoin the race. This is all done in under 10 seconds. Teams practice for many hours—a pit stop could mean the difference between winning and losing.

STATS AND FACTS

YEARS OF PRODUCTION **2008**
ENGINE SIZE **2.4 liter**
NUMBER OF CYLINDERS **8**
TRANSMISSION **Semiautomatic**
GEARBOX **7-speed**
0–62 MPH (0–100 KPH) **2 seconds**
TOP SPEED **205 mph (330 kph)**
WEIGHT **1,334 lb. (605 kg)—incl. driver**
CO_2 EMISSIONS (G/KM) **Not available**
FUEL ECONOMY
1.3 mpg (217 L/100 km)

M1

The M1 was developed by BMW in collaboration with the Italian manufacturer Lamborghini. The car was designed to be driven in endurance races, in which cars drive as far as they can in a set number of hours.

Each M1 car was built by hand, and only 455 of them were ever made. Racing enthusiasts still race M1 cars today, decades after the last one drove off the production line.

Amazing Design

To celebrate the 30th anniversary of the first M1, BMW designed the concept car, M1 Homage. The design takes the M1's wedge shape and updates it using the latest technology to see what it would look like if it were made today. It has the M1's distinctive kidney-shaped twin grilles, which channel air over the front brakes to keep them cool.

STATS AND FACTS

YEARS OF PRODUCTION **1978–81**
ENGINE SIZE **3.6 liter**
NUMBER OF CYLINDERS **6**
TRANSMISSION **Manual (Stick shift)**
GEARBOX **5-speed**
0–62 MPH (0–100 KPH) **5.5 seconds**
TOP SPEED **162 mph (260 kph)**
WEIGHT **2,866 lb. (1,300 kg)**
CO_2 EMISSIONS (G/KM) **Not available**
FUEL ECONOMY
14.4 mpg (19.6 L/100 km)

Procar

In 1979 and 1980, BMW ran a series of races called the Procar Championship, in which drivers competed against each other in M1 cars. The Championship was a pure test of driver skill. Many Formula 1 drivers took part, including Niki Lauda and Nelson Piquet, who relished the opportunity of racing each other in identical cars.

BMW first asked an artist to paint their racing cars in 1975. The cars became known as the Art Cars. This is the M1 Art Car that competed in the 1979 Le Mans race. It was painted by the American artist Andy Warhol.

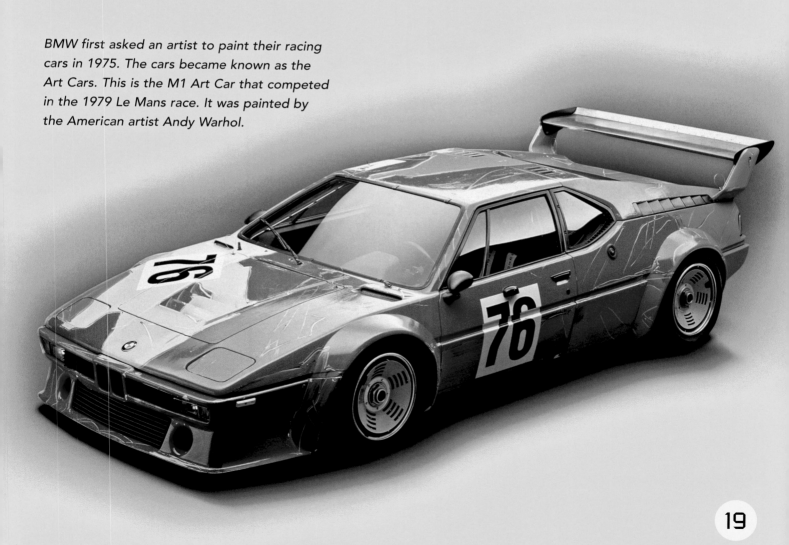

→Other Racing

In addition to its Formula 1 team, BMW organizes its own racing championship, known as Formula BMW.

Formula BMW is the first step up from karting in a young driver's career. Competitors as young as 15 can take part. BMW also enters cars in Touring Car championships, where production cars that have been adapted for racing drive against each other.

Formula BMW

In Formula BMW, all competitors drive the same single-seater FB02 car. Three separate series are held, in Europe, the Americas, and Asia. The best drivers from these three regions then compete in the World Final. Promising drivers are given sponsorship to develop their skills, and each year's winner is invited to test drive for the BMW Sauber Formula 1 team. The Formula 1 star Sebastian Vettel started his career in this way.

Amazing Design

BMW race the 320si in the World Touring Car Championship. A racing 320 looks different from one used for ordinary road driving. The chassis is the same, but the engine, suspension, brakes, and wheels are all different. There is just one seat for the driver, who sits inside a specially built safety cage that gives extra protection in a crash.

steering wheel customized to suit the driver's height and arm length

head and neck support system

6-point safety belt straps driver firmly into their seat

STATS AND FACTS

FB02

YEARS OF PRODUCTION **2002**
ENGINE SIZE **1.2 liter**
NUMBER OF CYLINDERS **4**
TRANSMISSION **Semiautomatic**
GEARBOX **6-speed**
0–62 MPH (0–100 KPH) **4 seconds**
TOP SPEED **143 mph (230 kph)**
WEIGHT **1,160 lb. (526 kg)**
CO_2 EMISSIONS (G/KM) **Not available**
FUEL ECONOMY
Not available

Models at a Glance

Model	Years Made	Numbers Built	Did You Know?
319/1	1934–36	178	A 319 could manage speeds of 80 mph (130 kph) with ease—common today but impressive in its time.
328	1937–39	464	One of the most successful sports cars of its day. In May 2008, a 328 sold in auction for $525,000.
507	1956–59	252	Elvis Presley owned a white 507 and gave it to Ursula Andress, James Bond film actress, in the 1960s.
E23 7 Series	1977–86	285,000	The first BMW model to be fitted with a "check control" system, ABS, and air conditioning.
M1	1978–81	455	As one of BMW's rarer models, an M1 in good condition can fetch over $150,000 today.
Z4 Roadster	2002–08 (second generation in production from 2009)	200,000 per year	The Z4 Roadster has one of the fastest retractable roofs in the world.
M6	2003–present	Approximately 4,000 per year	With the speed limiter removed, an M6 could reach speeds of 205 mph (330 kph).
M3	2005–present	Unknown. Limited by number of engines built	The E30 M3 has won more road races than any other BMW model in history.
320si	2005–present	2,600 per year	The engine has been hand built to a special design that reduces the number of moving parts.

Lamborghini

Published in 2011 by The Rosen Publishing Group Inc.
29 East 21st Street, New York, NY 10010

First Edition

Editor: Camilla Lloyd
Produced by Tall Tree Ltd
Editor, Tall Tree: Emma Marriott
Designer: Jonathan Vipond

Library of Congress Cataloging-in-Publication Data

Colson, Rob Scott.
  Lamborghini / by Rob Scott Colson. -- 1st ed.
      p. cm. -- (Ultimate cars)
  ISBN 978-1-4488-3087-9 (trade paperback Lamborghini/BMW)
  1. Lamborghini automobile--Juvenile literature. I. Title.
  TL215.L33C6385 2011
  629.222'2--dc22

                                      2009045422

Photographs
All images Automobili Lamborghini Holding
S.p.A., except: 4 Geoff du Feu / Alamy

Manufactured in China
CPSIA Compliance Information: Batch #WAS0102PK: For Further Information
contact Rosen Publishing, New York, New York at 1-800-237-9932

ULTIMATE CARS

Lamborghini

Rob Scott Colson

PowerKiDS press™

New York

Lamborghini

The Lamborghini car company was founded in 1963 by Ferruccio Lamborghini, a tractor manufacturer who collected sports cars. He thought that all his cars had something wrong with their design.

Ferruccio decided he would build "a very normal, but perfect" sports car. But many of the cars his company have made have been far from normal. They are some of the fastest cars ever allowed on the road.

Lamborghini made his fortune selling tractors such as this one, which is used to clean beaches in Tunisia.

Ferruccio Lamborghini sits on his personal Lamborghini, a Jarama GTS, outside the tractor factory in the early 1970s.

Amazing Design

At the end of World War II, a young Ferruccio Lamborghini (1916–93) started making tractors out of abandoned military vehicles. By the 1960s, he was a rich man who owned many expensive cars. He wasn't happy with the Ferrari he owned, so he ordered his engineers to take it apart and see what was wrong with it. It was then that he decided he could make better cars himself.

Charging Bull

The Lamborghini logo is a golden bull. It was chosen to represent Ferruccio Lamborghini's birth sign, Taurus the bull. Many of the company's cars have been named after famous bulls from bullfights in Spain. Lamborghini thought that the name of a fierce bull was a good match for his fast cars.

The charging bull is golden yellow. Many Lamborghinis are painted the same color.

Murciélago

The Murciélago is a maximum-performance sports car, which means that it can reach very fast speeds and accelerate (increase speed) very quickly.

The latest model of the Murciélago is the LP640. The LP640 is available as a coupé with a fixed roof, and as a roadster with a removable roof. The coupé version is featured here.

Every part of the body is designed to be as aerodynamic as possible.

Amazing Design

When a car moves, it needs to force the air in front of it out of the way. This causes drag—a combination of air resistance and friction between the car and the air, which slows the car down. The Murciélago's "wedge" shape is aerodynamic because it allows the car to cut a path through the air at high speeds, reducing drag. This shape was originally developed for fighter jets.

The engine's 12 cylinders are arranged in two groups of six in a "V" shape.

STATS AND FACTS

YEARS OF
PRODUCTION
2006–present
ENGINE SIZE **6.5 liter**
NUMBER OF CYLINDERS **12**
TRANSMISSION **Manual (Stick shift)**
GEARBOX **6-speed**
0–62 MPH (0–100 KPH) **3.4 seconds**
TOP SPEED **211 mph (340 kph)**
WEIGHT **3,671 lb. (1,665 kg)**
CO_2 EMISSIONS (G/KM) **495**
FUEL ECONOMY **13.2 mpg**
(21.3 L/100 km)

Engine

The Murciélago has an enormous 6.5-liter engine— four times bigger than the engine of a normal family car. This powerful engine is cooled by a Variable Air-flow Cooling System, which opens to let air in from outside the car during hot conditions.

Reventón

This is a car for millionaires—literally—since it costs $1.5 million. It has the same engine as the Murciélago, but is modeled even more closely on fighter jets.

In 2007, a Reventón raced against a Tornado jet plane on a 1.86 mile (3 km) long runway in Brescia, Italy. The car led the race almost to the end, but the jet fighter passed it in the last few yards.

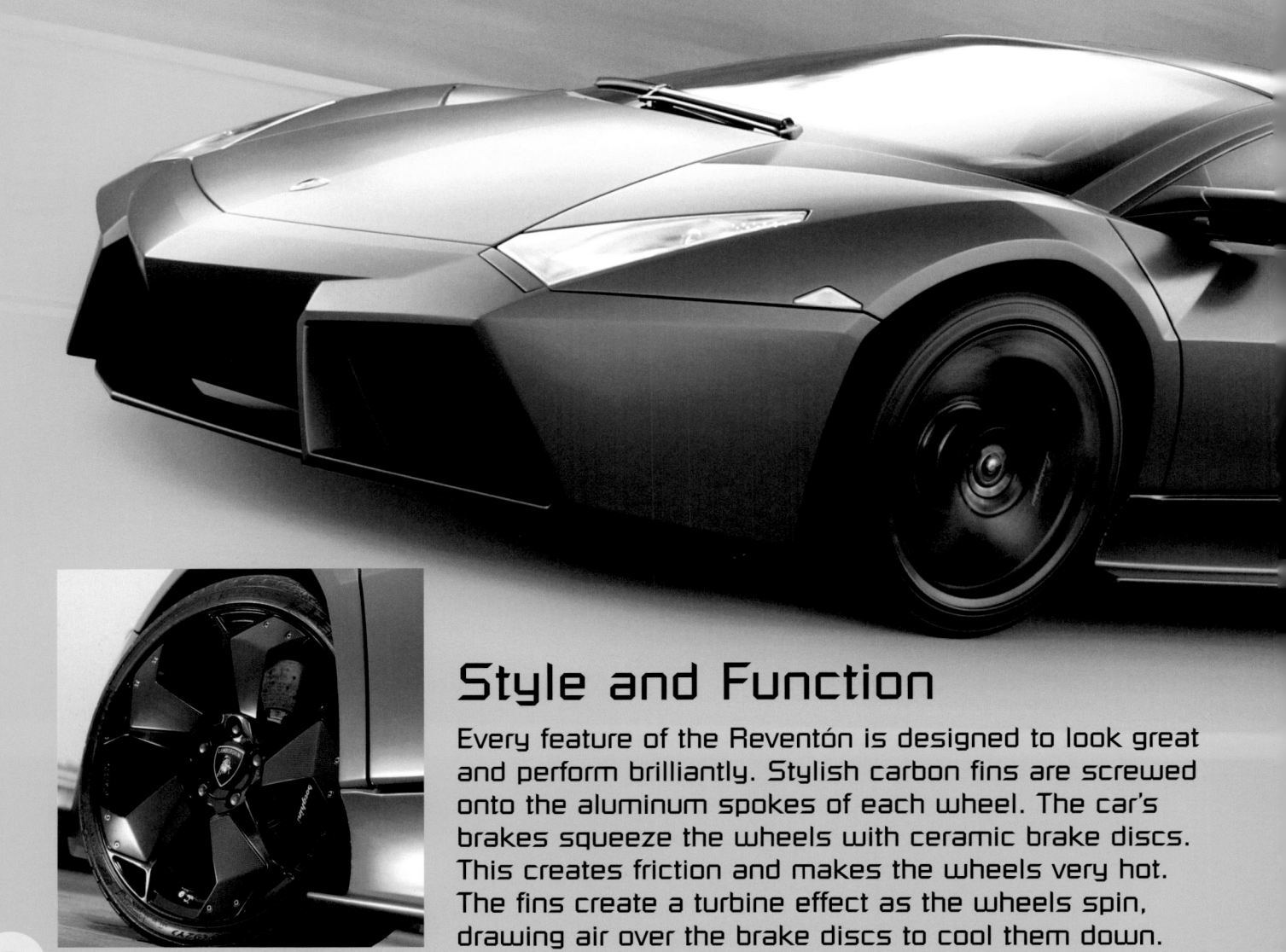

Style and Function

Every feature of the Reventón is designed to look great and perform brilliantly. Stylish carbon fins are screwed onto the aluminum spokes of each wheel. The car's brakes squeeze the wheels with ceramic brake discs. This creates friction and makes the wheels very hot. The fins create a turbine effect as the wheels spin, drawing air over the brake discs to cool them down.

G-Force Meter shows the stresses on the car as it takes corners.

Screens to left and right display essential information such as speed and fuel levels.

Amazing Design

Three liquid crystal displays inside the car show a variety of information from the on-board computer to the driver. The screen in the middle, known as the G-Force Meter, is unique to the Reventón. On a 3-D grid, the meter shows the gravitational forces as the car accelerates or goes around bends. This means that the driver knows at all times exactly what stress the car is under. Both Formula 1 cars and aircraft use similar instruments to ensure that drivers or pilots do not lose control at high speeds.

The Reventón is a very exclusive car. Just 21 cars have been made—one for the Lamborghini museum and 20 for sale. Each one is stamped inside with its own number between 0 and 20.

Side air intakes help to cool the ceramic brake discs.

STATS AND FACTS

YEARS OF PRODUCTION
2008–present
ENGINE SIZE **6.5 liter**
NUMBER OF CYLINDERS **12**
TRANSMISSION **Manual (Stick shift)**
GEARBOX **6-speed**
0–62 MPH (0–100 KPH) **3.4 seconds**
TOP SPEED **211 (340 kph)**
WEIGHT **3,671 lb. (1,665 kg)**
CO_2 EMISSIONS (G/KM) **495**
FUEL ECONOMY
13.2 mpg (21.3 L/100 km)

Gallardo Spyder

The Gallardo was first produced in 2003 as a coupé, a car with a fixed, hard roof. In 2006, Lamborghini produced the Gallardo Spyder, which has a soft roof.

The Spyder's chassis (the car's "skeleton") has been reinforced (made stronger) to make up for its lack of a hard roof. This change means that it is a little heavier and slower than the coupé.

Retracting Roof

The roof of the Gallardo Spyder can be removed at the touch of a button. The engine cover lifts up and the soft top folds back into a space next to the engine behind the seats. The engine cover and the soft roof are both controlled by rams—rods that move out and in. The rams are hydraulic, which means that they are powered by liquid under pressure.

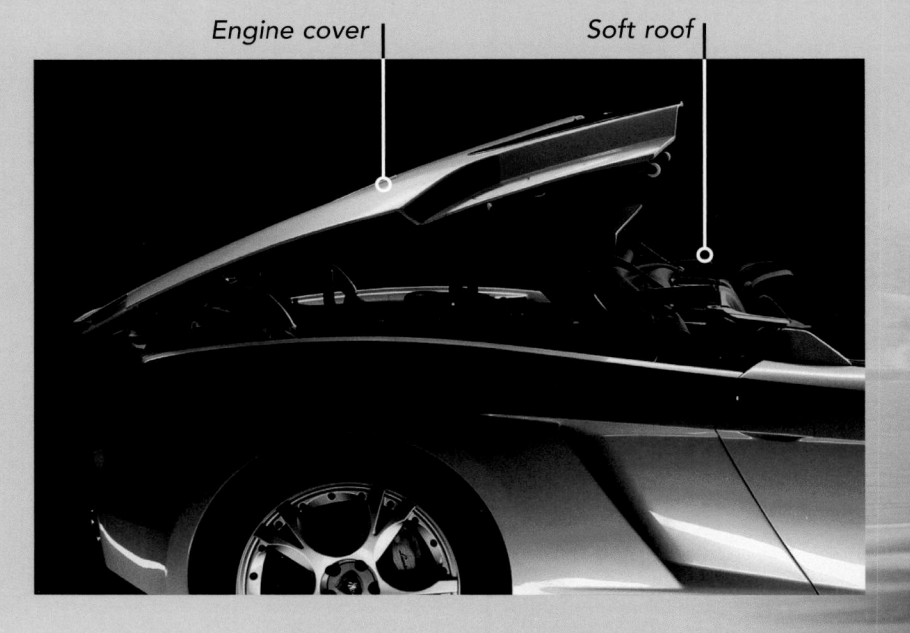

Engine cover | Soft roof

STATS AND FACTS

Years
of production
2006–present
Engine size **5 liter**
Number of cylinders **10**
Transmission **Semiautomatic**
Gearbox **6-speed**
0–62 mph (0–100 kph) **4.3 seconds**
Top speed **195 mph (314 kph) roof closed;
191 mph (307 kph) roof open**
Weight **3,461 lb. (1,570 kg)**
CO_2 Emissions (g/km) **400**
Fuel economy
15.6 mpg (18.1 L/100 km)

The chassis is made of a space frame—a lightweight structure of metal rods fixed to each other in a grid pattern.

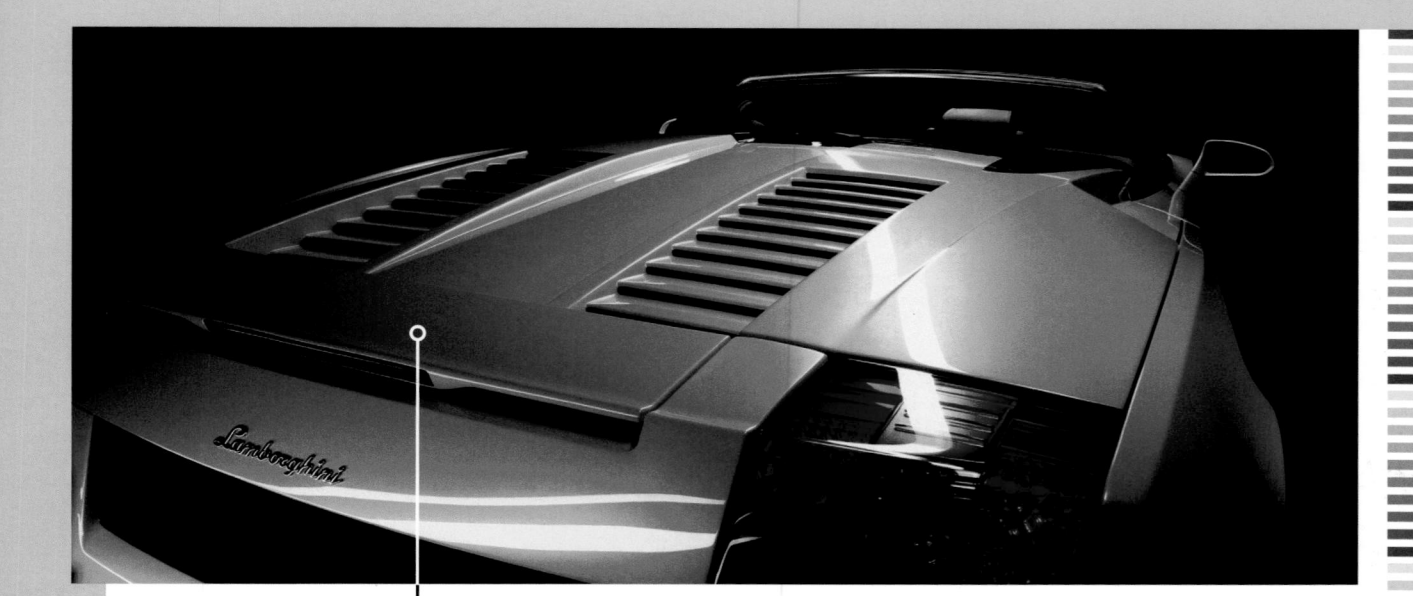

Amazing Design

The spoiler lies flat against the trunk at low speeds.

The Gallardo has the distinctive Lamborghini wedge shape that is so aerodynamic, it is in danger of taking off at high speed! To solve this problem, the rear spoiler (a bar at the back of the car) automatically rises up when the car's speed reaches 75 mph (120 kph). The spoiler disrupts (spoils) the flow of air over the car, producing downforce that keeps the wheels safely on the road.

350 GT

The 350 was Lamborghini's first car. It was called this because its engine was 350 cubic centimeters (21.4 cu. in.).

The 350 produced to sell to the public was called the 350 GT. Only 120 350 GTs were ever made, but it is the car that established Lamborghini as a new and exciting car manufacturer.

Amazing Design

One of the most amazing parts of the 350's design cannot be seen from the outside. The chassis was made using a frame of thin metal tubes. The tubes were then covered in aluminum panels. Most cars at that time were made using thicker tubes. The technique was called *superleggera* (an Italian word meaning "super light"), and it made the car lighter and faster.

GT stands for "grand tourer"—a high-performance car designed to be driven over long distances.

The very first 350 was called the GTV. It was a prototype—a model made to show how the design would work. It looked the part but it did not have an engine!

Dream Team

One of the keys to the 350's success was the team behind it. Its chief engineer, Giotto Bizzarrini, had been chief designer for the rival Italian company, Ferrari. The designer, Gian Paolo Dallara, later went on to found his own company, and makes the chassis for all IndyCar racing cars today.

STATS AND FACTS

YEARS
OF PRODUCTION
1964–66
ENGINE SIZE **3.5 liter**
NUMBER OF CYLINDERS **12**
TRANSMISSION **Manual (Stick shift)**
GEARBOX **5-speed**
0–62 MPH (0–100 KPH) **6.5 seconds**
TOP SPEED **155 mph (250 kph)**
WEIGHT **2,645 lb. (1,200 kg)**
CO_2 EMISSIONS (G/KM) **Not available**
FUEL ECONOMY
Not available

Miura

The Miura replaced the 350 GT, and was the first Lamborghini model to have a name inspired by bullfighting. The Miura was named after a Spanish breeder of fighting bulls called Antonio Miura. It had a larger engine than the 350, and could go 19 mph (30 kph) faster.

The engines in the very first Miuras would sometimes catch on fire when the car accelerated, but once they had fixed this dangerous problem, it became a hugely successful model.

Unusually, the Miura's hood opens down the middle. The front and rear panels open up like a clamshell.

Amazing Design

The Miura was one of the first two-seater road cars to have the engine in the middle of the car rather than at the front. This spread the car's weight and made it easier to control at high speed. Before the Miura, only racing cars had been made this way. It was not surprising that the Miura was the fastest street-legal car of its time.

Lamborghini improved the engine in later models, making them even faster.

Only one Miura Roadster was ever made, but some owners have converted their Miuras to look like it.

Open Top

In 1968, Lamborghini built a roadster version of the Miura. Only one was ever made. It does not have a removable roof like the Gallardo Spyder. In fact, it does not have a roof at all. This one-of-a-kind car was shown at car shows, but it was decided not to make any more—possibly because its owners would want to be able to drive in the rain, too!

STATS AND FACTS

YEARS OF PRODUCTION **1966–72**
ENGINE SIZE **3.9 liter**
NUMBER OF CYLINDERS **12**
TRANSMISSION **Manual (Stick shift)**
GEARBOX **5-speed**
0–62 MPH (0–100 KPH) **6.7 seconds**
TOP SPEED **174 mph (280 kph)**
WEIGHT **2,848 lb. (1,292 kg)**
CO_2 EMISSIONS (G/KM) **Not available**
FUEL ECONOMY
14 mpg (19 L/100 km)

Countach

The Countach was the first Lamborghini to be designed with the now-familiar wedge shape.

The shape was the idea of designer Marcello Gandini. It looks very sleek, but its sharp corners are in fact not as aerodynamic as Lamborghini's later wedge-shaped cars, whose designers used wind tunnels and computers to perfect the shape.

Lamborghini have attached "scissor" doors to all their wedge-shaped cars.

Amazing Design

At just over 6.5 feet (2 m) across, the Countach is 8–12 in. (20–30 cm) wider than most road cars, which could cause problems on narrow streets. Its "scissor" doors open up rather than out, like a bird raising its wings, so there is room to climb in and out. The doors swing open from a hinge at the front—an arrangement known as a "jack-knife."

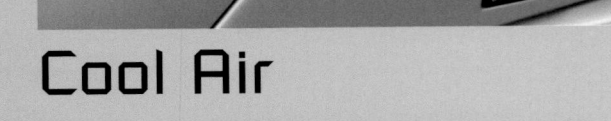

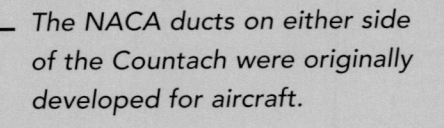

The NACA ducts on either side of the Countach were originally developed for aircraft.

Cool Air

Lamborghini changed the Countach when they discovered that the engine in the prototype was overheating. They added large side vents to keep the engine cool. The vents are known as NACA (National Advisory Panel for Aeronautics) ducts. The ducts do not stick out, so they allow air to be drawn in over the engine without damaging the car's aerodynamics.

The Countach made the sharp-angled style popular.

STATS AND FACTS

YEARS OF PRODUCTION **1974–89**
ENGINE SIZE **3.9 liter**
NUMBER OF CYLINDERS **12**
TRANSMISSION **Manual (Stick shift)**
GEARBOX **5-speed**
0–62 MPH (0–100 KPH) **5.9 seconds**
TOP SPEED **186 mph (300 kph)**
WEIGHT **2,645 lb. (1,200 kg)**
CO_2 EMISSIONS (G/KM) **Not available**
FUEL ECONOMY **11 mpg (25.7 L/100 km)**

Diablo

The Countach was designed for style. But the model that replaced it, the Diablo, was made for speed.

Its name suits it well—*diablo* is the Spanish word for "devil," and this car can go devilishly fast. It is also devilishly noisy, and you are likely to hear a Diablo long before you see it. Its engine roars at over 100 decibels—as loud as your MP3 player turned up to full volume.

Amazing Design

The cockpit of the Diablo is pushed forward to allow room for the enormous 6-liter engine that sits behind it. This means there is not much leg room for the driver or passenger. There are also very few luxuries in the Diablo as each new gadget would add weight to the car and reduce its speed. With a top speed of 210 mph (338 kph), the Diablo could give a Formula 1 car a very good race.

Racing Devil

In 1994, to celebrate the 30th anniversary of Lamborghini's first car, the company made a special racing version of the Diablo known as the SE30. The SE30 had even fewer luxuries than the standard Diablo. It had no radio, air conditioning, or sound insulation and was fitted with carbon fiber seats. This made it 275 lb. (125 kg) lighter than the standard model—a thrilling, if noisy, hot, and uncomfortable drive.

In 1999, Lamborghini redesigned the body of the Diablo slightly and gave it a bigger engine. The result was the Diablo GT, the fastest sports car in the world at the time.

STATS AND FACTS

Years of production **1990–2001**
Engine size **6 liter**
Number of cylinders **12**
Transmission **Manual (Stick shift)**
Gearbox **5-speed**
0–62 mph (0–100 kph) **3.5 seconds**
Top speed **210 mph (338 kph)**
Weight **3,219 lb. (1,460 kg)**
CO_2 Emissions (g/km) **Not available**
Fuel economy **12 mpg (24 L/100 km)**

Racing

Perhaps surprisingly for a manufacturer of some of the fastest cars ever made, Ferruccio Lamborghini decided that motor racing was too expensive.

After Ferrucio retired, the company became involved in Formula 1 as an engine supplier. Finally, after Lamborghini's death, racing models of the Diablo competed in the Diablo Supertrophy, a race series that was held from 1996 to 1999.

A racing Diablo, the first car made entirely by Lamborghini to compete on the track.

Formula 1

In Lamborghini's first two seasons in Formula 1, 1989 and 1990, they supplied engines to two teams—Larrousse and Lotus. Their results improved steadily to a best finish of fourth. In 1991, Lamborghini funded a new team, Modena, who disappeared after one season. Their experiment with Formula 1 ended two years later.

Cylinders

Amazing Design

Lamborghini developed the powerful 12-cylinder, 3.5-liter engine used in Formula 1 in partnership with the U.S. company, Chrysler. However, the continuous changes that Formula 1 demands, as the drivers push the cars to their limits, proved too expensive for Lamborghini.

Engine block—a solid frame in which the cylinders pump up and down.

Models at a Glance

Model	Years Made	Numbers Built	Did You Know?
350 GT	1964–66	120	As Lamborghini's pioneering model, the 350 GT provided Ferrari with a serious Italian competitor.
Miura	1966–72	764	With its mid-engined layout, this trend-leading car set the standard for two-seater, high-performance cars.
Jarama	1970–76	328	Created for the "gentleman," this was one of Ferruccio Lamborghini's favorite models.
Countach	1974–89	2,042	Its innovative wedge-shape body is only 3.5 ft. (1.07 m) tall—a design that redefined the look of sports cars.
Diablo	1990–2001	3,000	In 1999, the Diablo GT was the world's fastest sports car with a top speed of 210 mph (338 kph).
Murciélago	2001–present	3,066 (at the end of 2007)	To show off its 6.5-liter engine, the LP640 can be supplied with a transparent glass engine hood.
Gallardo	2003–present	6,801 (at the end of 2007)	The LP 560-4 Spyder takes only 4 seconds to sprint from 0 to 62 mph (0 to 100 kph).
Reventón	2008–present	21 (at the end of 2008)	The on-board computer features the G-Force Meter that is also used by aircraft and is unique to this model.